ONE DIRECTION

Take Me Home

Mary Boone

TRIUMPH
BOOKS

This book is available in quantity at special discounts for your group or organization. For further information, contact:

Triumph Books LLC
814 North Franklin Street
Chicago, Illinois 60610
Phone: (312) 337-0747
www.triumphbooks.com

Printed in U.S.A.

ISBN: 978-1-60078-901-4

Content developed and packaged by Rockett Media, Inc.
Writer: Mary Boone
Editor: Bob Baker
Design: Andrew Burwell
Page production: Chad Bell
Cover design by Andrew Burwell

Photographs courtesy of Getty Images unless otherwise noted

ONE DIRECTION

Take Me Home

CHAPTER ONE
FIVE HANDSOME GUYS, ONE MUSICAL SENSATION

In two years, you could learn the basics of a foreign language, grow your hair a foot longer or – if you're Niall Horan, Zayn Malik, Liam Payne, Harry Styles and Louis Tomlinson – you could achieve worldwide fame.

Since placing third on *The X Factor*, the guys of One Direction have set sales records, shown up on the covers of dozens of magazines, and melted the hearts of millions of girls and young women around the globe.

These five well-coiffed cuties may be the most famous "losers" that *The X Factor* has ever produced.

Most fans know the story, but a quick recap:

These five guys – total strangers – auditioned for 2010's *The X Factor*. They made it through the earliest rounds of competition but were cut when they got to the boot camp stage.

The judges – Simon Cowell, Louis Walsh and Nicole Scherzinger – talked it over. These guys were good. Should they really be eliminated? In a dramatic reality TV move, four girls, along with Harry, Liam, Louis, Niall and Zayn, were called back onto the stage. If the guys performed together as one group and the girls performed as a second group, they could all continue to compete. Were they interested? You bet!

The guys quickly shifted gears. No longer solo competitors, they needed to learn to perform as a group. Initially, it was tough to share ideas and they didn't have a clue about harmonizing.

Fortunately, that awkward stage didn't last long and, with the aid of intense rehearsal and coaching, they were able to sail through early competition and then onto the live shows, mentored by *The X Factor* creator Simon Cowell.

As the guys developed skills and confidence, they quickly attracted a huge fan base.

"Normally when you put together a band they have some time to go away and develop but we had to do that in a live

competition, in front of 20 million people," says Liam. "If you make a mistake in front of an audience like that, you get voted out. We had no room for error whatsoever. We had to grow up very, very fast."

During the 10 weeks of live shows, One Direction covered songs ranging

from Bryan Adams' "Summer of '69" and Coldplay's "Viva La Vida" to Kelly Clarkson's "My Life Would Suck Without You" and Snow Patrol's "Chasing Cars." Thanks to their very solid performances,

they became the first manufactured group to make it through the show's first nine weeks of on-air competition.

In the show's final episode, the band performed Elton John's "Your Song," World Party's "She's the One" (with pop superstar Robbie Williams) and Natalie Imbruglia's "Torn."

Matt Cardle won *The X Factor* that year, followed by runner-up Rebecca Ferguson. One Direction's third-place finish, however, has not harmed their career in any way.

In fact, on March 22, 2012, One Direction became the first UK group ever to debut at No. 1 on the U.S. *Billboard 200* album chart, a feat they accomplished by knocking recording stars Bruce Springsteen and Adele each down a notch. The previous highest entry for a UK group's first album was No. 6, when the Spice Girls entered the U.S. charts with "Spice" in 1997.

In a statement released by the group's record label, Niall noted: "When we got put together as a group, we couldn't

EVEN IDOLS HAVE IDOLS

Every generation has had its teen music idols and the guys of One Direction have certainly achieved that status. They have all the prerequisites: their photos on magazine covers, frenzied fans chasing their bus, paparazzi posses.

Even though they've achieved worldwide fame, the guys are quick to point out that they still get a little weak in the knees when they meet certain famous people – the idols they've long admired from afar.

Louis Tomlinson says his admiration for English singer-songwriter Robbie Williams began years ago.

"I've always loved Robbie," Louis told *Now* magazine. "He's just so cheeky, he can get away with anything. His performances are unbelievable."

Louis says of all the celebrities he met on *The X Factor*, Robbie was one of the kindest. "We hung out with him. He's a really cool guy."

When pressed to name his musical idol, **Harry Styles** was quick with his answer: English singer-songwriter Chris Martin.

"My biggest idol has always been Chris Martin from Coldplay," Harry revealed in an interview for Tumblr's 2012 Storyboard project. "He is such a great singer, performer and writer. If I could be as talented as any musician, it would be him all day long."

Zayn Malik was so uneasy about meeting one of his idols – actor Johnny Depp – that he skipped out on the opportunity.

Back in November 2012, when the band had a chance to spend time with the *Pirates of the Caribbean* star and his daughter, Lily-Rose, Zayn took a pass, saying he needed to stay behind and Skype with his girlfriend.

Later, Zayn admitted his decision to skip the meeting was fear driven.

"I am a massive, massive fan and I didn't want to embarrass myself, so I let the boys go without me," he told *The (London) Mirror*. "Hopefully, there will be a next time. The boys said he was totally cool."

"Some of our fans get so excited or nervous when they meet us and that's how I was at the thought of being with Johnny."

Around the same time the guys were meeting Mr. Depp, **Liam Payne** got to meet Jay-Z. Liam snapped a photo of himself with the rapper/record producer at the Brooklyn, N.Y., stop of Justin Bieber's Believe Tour and tweeted: "Alssoooo my biggest news todayy i met one of my idols and couldnt even look him in the eye..."

The 1D guys have made no secret that they'd love to work with Beyonce's better half.

"I would love to do a hip-hop collaboration with Jay-Z," Liam told MTV News. "I don't know how to talk to him, though. I think he's wicked. I love Jay-Z. It upsets me that we're not cool enough, but I wish we could."

Niall Horan says he completely understands what it's like to be starstruck because he got pretty excited himself

Niall Horan was starstruck when he met singer Michael Bublé.

when he bumped into one of his favorite stars: Canadian crooner Michael Bublé. Niall and the guys bumped into Michael in November 2012 in Los Angeles.

Niall has made no secret of his crush on Bublé. "I have a man crush on Michael Bublé, he's the man! He's all I have on my iPod," he told *The News Of The World*.

When Niall finally had a chance to meet his idol, he snapped a quick photo and tweeted: "Look who I met in the airport yesterday! @michaelBublé."

Niall confesses the meeting left him in awe, telling Nickelodeon: "I'm new to the game. I find it hard to keep my emotions inside. When I met Michael Bublé, he's like my idol, so I kinda flipped out."

imagine ourselves coming to America, let alone releasing our album here, so for us to be sitting at the top of the U.S. album charts is unbelievable."

Within the first week of its release, One Direction sold more than 176,000 copies of its debut album, "Up All Night." The CD shot straight to the top of the digital charts within minutes of its official release on March 13, 2012. Four months later, the band was honored by Syco Music and Sony Music for having 12 million in worldwide sales in less than a year.

Of course, One Direction's popularity is not solely defined by record sales or screaming fans.

By March 2013, the band's group and individual Twitter accounts had a combined

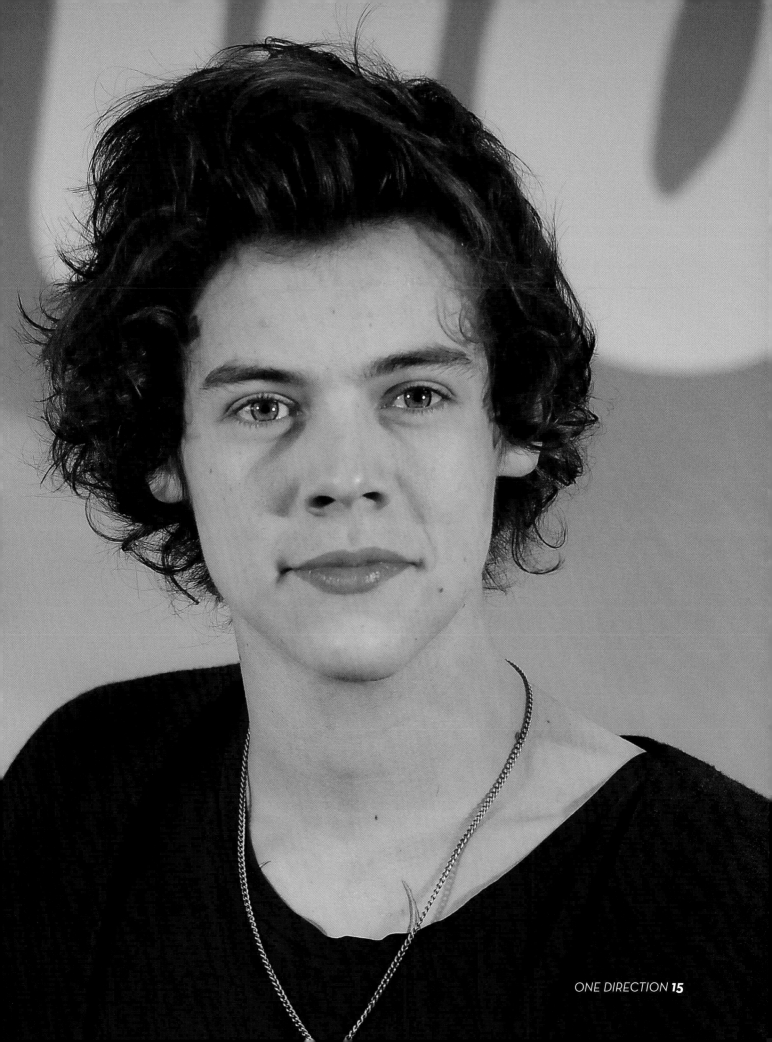

NIALL

59.6 million followers. They'd accumulated nearly 14 million "likes" on their official Facebook page and most shows on their 2013 World Tour sold out more than a year ahead of time.

The guys' fame came quickly but they insist it hasn't changed them.

In fact, Liam suggests much of their success is due to the fact that they're just normal guys and the best of friends.

"For us, the main thing is we've just been ourselves," Liam told ContactMusic.com in November 2012. "Lots of people get into our situation and you hear that they've changed. We've just stayed as ourselves. There's a lot of things the fans don't know about us. People still ask whether we really get on or not – and we genuinely do. A lot of people don't believe that."

Here's a quick look at One Direction's five uniquely talented – but chummy – members:

On Twitter: @NiallOfficial

The basics: Niall, the only Irish member of One Direction, describes himself as the group's most "carefree" member. In addition to being a talented vocalist, Niall plays the guitar.

Earliest performances: As young as four, he

NIALL JAMES HORAN

Birthdate: September 13, 1993
Hometown: Mullinger, Westmeath, Ireland

was singing "Saturday Night at the Movies" to anyone who would listen. Niall began his theatrical "career" in a production of "Oliver!" at St. Kenny National School,

THE MAN BEHIND ONE DIRECTION

Simon Cowell can't sing or even read music. So, how has he managed to become one of the most successful people in the music industry?

"(I) guess what's going to be popular," he told interviewer Anderson Cooper in 2007.

The ability to "guess" has served him well. He's at the helm of successful companies in both Great Britain and the United States, and gained considerable notoriety as the acerbic judge on *The X Factor, Britain's Got Talent, American Idol* and *X Factor USA.* In addition to his hit TV shows, Cowell is a record executive for Sony BMG.

The son of a music industry executive and socialite/ballet dancer, Cowell got early exposure to the entertainment world. He dropped out of school at age 16 and worked odd jobs until his father got him a job with EMI Music Publishing. He started off doing errands and worked his way up the ladder until he got a job at EMI as a record producer. He eventually left that company to start his own small record labels. He later joined BMG where he helped launch the bands Five and Westlife.

His Syco label signed the top two finishers of the first season of *Pop Idol,* Will Young and Gareth Gates, both of whom went on to score No. 1 hits in the United Kingdom. More recently, his musical "creations" include the group Il Divo, a multinational operatic pop group that, to date, has sold more than 26 million albums worldwide.

Cowell signed One Direction to a $2.98 million contract with his Syco Records label after the group finished third in the seventh season of the British television singing competition *The X Factor* in 2010.

Cowell (or "Mr Growl" as 1D have affectionately nicknamed him) told *Rolling Stone* he was impressed with the guys from the moment he met them on *The X Factor* – but they were solo artists then. Once he and the other judges invited them to continue in the competition as a group, their collective success seemed more certain.

"The minute they stood there for the first time together – it was a weird feeling. They just looked like a group at that point," he said. "I had a good feeling, but then obviously we had about a five-week wait where they had to work together. They had to come back for another section of the show where they performed together as a group for the first time. I was concerned whether five weeks was long enough, but they came back five weeks later and were absolutely sensational."

where he was often selected to sing solos with the school choir.

On touring: Niall adores it. "I love it," he told *Vogue* in December 2012. "I love the screaming. They love it, too: they've all got their tickets and they've been waiting a year or so to see you, so you've got to give it your best."

Going green: Niall insists that, when it comes to girls, he doesn't really have a "type." He told interviewer Ryan Seacrest: "I like someone that's cute. Someone that can have a good time, have a lot of fun and someone that I share a lot of interests with." That said, the blonde singer admits he has "a soft spot for girls with green eyes."

ZAYN

ZAYN JAWAAD MALIK

Birthdate: January 12, 1993
Hometown: West Lane Baildon, Bradford, England
On Twitter: @zaynmalik1D

The basics: Born to a British Pakistani father and English mother, Zayn says his mixed heritage initially made it difficult to fit in at school. He began taking a keen interest in his appearance when he turned 12; that new-found pride in his appearance led to increased confidence and a better attitude. He has a reputation as 1D's most vain member.

Earliest performances: He sang with school choirs and had roles in a couple of school musicals. In 2010, he took the gigantic leap from singing in his bedroom

to auditioning for *The X Factor*. His audition song was Mario's "Let Me Love You."

Sketch factor: Zayn's a talented artist and received credit for some of the illustrations on the group's debut CD. His sketches are not always appreciated by his bandmates, especially when he creates caricatures of them with funny hair or big ears.

Eyes have it: Zayn is "very attracted to a girl's eyes. They don't have to be a certain color. I think you can tell a lot by a girl's eyes."

LIAM JAMES PAYNE

Birthdate: August 29, 1993
Hometown: Wolverhampton, England
On Twitter: @Real_Liam_Payne
The basics: Liam auditioned for *The X Factor* as a 14-year-old and made it through to the judges' houses. That time around, the

judges decided he was simply too young and advised him to try again in a couple years; thank goodness he did. Sometimes described as "Papa Smurf," Liam is smart, sensible and considered the father figure in the group.

Earliest performances: Liam made his first public performance at age five, singing a rendition of Robbie Williams' "Let Me Entertain You" in a holiday camp competition. As a kid, he took classes at Pink Productions, a Wolverhampton-based performing arts school. He was studying musical technology in college when he entered *The X Factor* competition in 2010.

Good sport: Liam was involved in a variety of sports. He excelled at cross-country running and boxing.

On the lookout: Liam and girlfriend Danielle Peazer have been together more than two years – on and off. During one of their recent breakups, Liam told a BBC

LIAM

ONE DIRECTION

HARRY

interviewer that he likes cute, shy girls he can laugh with. More specifically, he said, he's looking for "Nice eyes, nice smile and good conversation."

HARRY EDWARD STYLES

Birthdate: February 1, 1994

Hometown: Holmes Chapel, Cheshire, England

On Twitter: @Harry_Styles

The basics: The youngest member of the group, Harry shares lead vocal duties with Liam. His reputation as a lady's man is well deserved; Harry has had very public relationships with women including singer/actress Caggie Dunlop, British TV personality Caroline Flack (15 years his senior), radio DJ Lucy Horobin (14 years his senior), actress Emily Atack, Canadian singer/songwriter Alyssa Reid, model Cara Delevingne, and American country/pop singer Taylor Swift.

Earliest performances: A long-time lover of karaoke, Harry participated in school plays at Holmes Chapel Comprehensive School. As a teen, his band, White Eskimo, won a battle of the bands competition.

Bad boy: Harry won the "Villain of the Year" prize at a 2013 awards ceremony sponsored by the British music publication *NME*. Among those he beat out for the award: Skrillex, PSY and British Prime Minister David Cameron.

His perfect match: Harry says he's looking for a curvy girl who is cute, kind,

loyal and has a good sense of humor. He also tells *Heat* magazine: "Most of my girlfriends have been blonde, but a good brunette is always nice."

LOUIS WILLIAM TOMLINSON

Birthdate: December 24, 1991

Hometown: Doncaster, South Yorkshire, England

On Twitter: @Louis_Tomlinson

The basics: Louis, the oldest member of One Direction, is also the prankster of the group.

Earliest performances: Louis got his first taste of the entertainment industry when he tagged along with his stepsisters who had roles on the TV drama *Fat Friends*. Soon after, he earned small roles in ITV's film *If I Had You* and BBC's *Waterloo Road*. He starred in several school productions before auditioning for *The X Factor*.

Safe, secure: In an effort to ensure he's safe from stalkers, thieves and kidnappers, Louis has reportedly shelled out more than $22,000 to have a "panic room" built in his home. These fortified rooms, designed to provide shelter in case of a home invasion or other threat, generally contain communications equipment so law enforcement authorities can be contacted.

Off the market: Louis and girlfriend Eleanor Calder met through Harry. Since he's not in the dating pool, he says he's happy to play the role of wingman. "Since I have a girlfriend, I'll start the night with her, but then I'll help out the guys by making them sound like the most incredible guys in the world," he told *Seventeen*.

LOUIS

CHAPTER TWO
FROM X FACTOR TO THE WORLD STAGE

The screams almost shattered the walls.

From the moment the lights went out and a countdown clock ticked down 5-4-3-2-1, Wolverhampton's Civic Hall was filled with ear-splitting teenage squeals.

But the girls were just getting warmed up. When Niall, Zayn, Harry, Louis and Wolverhampton's Liam Payne bounded on to the stage just seconds later, the volume level exploded, fans leapt to their feet and a million camera phones burst into life.

You could forgive Simon Cowell's boys for looking more than a little overwhelmed.

After all, this was the first gig of their first tour and for a few brief moments, all they could mouth was "wow."

— From *The (Wolverhampton) Express & Star*

AIR FORCE ONE DIRECTION

How do young pop stars know when they've made it big? Maybe it's when they score their first No. 1 hit? Their first magazine cover? Their first big concert tour?

For Harry Styles, Niall Horan, Zayn Malik, Liam Payne and Louis Tomlinson, that moment may have come when they got their very own private jet.

An EntertainmentWise.com report released on Jan. 1, 2013, revealed that the boys' label purchased the $1.36 million jet for them. It's been reported that the luxury plane is just for the 1D members, and that if they want friends or girlfriends to travel on tour with them they will have to find their own transportation.

Of course, One Direction is hardly the only act to have a private jet. Actors John Travolta, Harrison Ford and Tom Cruise, media mogul Oprah Winfrey, and musicians Rihanna, Justin Bieber, Celine Dion and Lady Gaga are among a growing number of entertainers who travel on their own planes, making it simpler to share their talents with the world.

One Direction's jet will whisk the guys around the globe for their 2013 tour, supposedly allowing more flexibility in their schedules and avoiding sometimes lengthy airport security lines. Band insignia on the plane will alert fans when the guys have landed in their city.

In reporting the aircraft news, the (London) Mirror paper immediately began referring to the plane as "Air Force One Direction" after the U.S. President's jet "Air Force One."

In addition to getting their own wings (as if that wasn't big enough), the guys also hired Michael Jackson's former bodyguard to accompany them on their 2013 world tour.

Just 2,000 fans attended One Direction's December 21, 2011, show in this West Midlands city – the first stop on their first headlining tour.

Sure, they'd done shows as part of the spring 2011 *X Factor* Live Tour, but that time around they were joined by nine other contestants from the reality TV series. This time, the pressure was theirs alone. Audience members had shelled out $30 to $42 each for tickets to see Niall Horan, Zayn Malik, Liam Payne, Harry Styles and Louis Tomlinson – the boys they'd fallen in love with on the telly.

Fans began lining up for that first show at 6:30 in the morning. Nine hours later, the throngs delighted when the guys arrived in two sleek silver Mercedes Viano vans. By the time the show finally began at 9 p.m., it was clear no one was going to leave the show disappointed.

The Wolverhampton show was the first of 21 that saw the band making stops at key European venues including London's HMV Apollo, Manchester's O2 Apollo, Liverpool's Echo Arena, Cardiff's Motorpoint Arena and the O2 in Dublin.

The guys entered that first headlining tour as stars. They left as superstars.

When One Direction made its first American television appearance on NBC's *Today* show on March 12, 2012, network executives were overwhelmed by the response. More than 10,000 adoring, screaming fans flocked to New York City's Rockefeller Plaza that day – the crowd was

OPENING ACT: CAMRYN

Camryn Magness is doing what millions of teenage girls only dream of doing. She's hanging out with the One Direction guys – night after night after night.

For her, "hanging out" is a little more formal than sitting on the sofa, watching TV. She's traveling with the band, opening the sold-out, 63-date European leg of their tour.

Camryn (in the music business, she's known only by her first name) opened for the guys during some of their 2012 shows and now she's back.

"It was amazing and terrifying," Camryn told CBSNews.com about warming up the crowd for One Direction. "It was the biggest audience I ever played to. So, going in there, I didn't really know what to expect. And I think that's the worst part – going in there, you don't know whether they're going to like you, or they're going to hate you. At the end of it all, it went amazing and I made a lot of new fans and friends."

Touring is not exactly new for Camryn. The Denver, Colo., native previously opened for Selena Gomez and, in 2011, she joined Cody Simpson and Greyson Chance on their Waiting 4U Tour. During the summer of 2011, Camryn toured the Midwestern United States with All Star Weekend, a pop band that gained fame from its appearances on the Disney Channel. During fall 2011, she launched a Back 2 School Tour, performing at nearly 100 schools and for more than 80,000 students.

Camryn is both excited and realistic about opening for 1D. She says she knows there's only one thing on every Directioner's mind when she steps up onstage to warm up the crowd.

"One Direction fans, usually when I walk out on stage I kind of go into thinking, 'Oh man, I'm a girl on their favorite boy band's tour; they hate me.' So I try to do my best to win them over," she told MTV News.

Camryn has been singing as long as she can remember and began entering talent shows when she was about seven years old. She recorded and started sending out demo records when she was just eight.

At the age of 10, Camryn recorded her first single, "Wait and See," with Frank Schooflar of the band Blessed By A Broken Heart and longtime family-friend Lennon Murphy.

Her first big break came in 2011, when director John Schultz selected "Wait and See" as the title track for his film adaptation of the children's book *Judy Moody and the Not Bummer Summer*. The song enjoyed moderate success, peaking at No. 38 on the *Billboard* charts.

Camryn's second single, "Set The Night On Fire," was written by Camryn, Frank Schooflar and Lennon Murphy. It debuted on Top 40 radio in the United States in May 2012.

Camryn, who is homeschooled, describes herself as self-motivated. "When I was eight, I decided that this is what I wanted to do," she told the *(Minneapolis) Star-Tribune* in April 2011.

Five Fun Facts About Camryn:

1. She comes from a show-biz family. Her parents are movie producers Gary Magness and Sarah Siegel-Magness who are best known for their 2009 Oscar-nominated film *Precious*.

2. Camryn's grandfather is Mo Siegel, the man behind Celestial Seasonings. Celestial Seasonings is one of the largest specialty tea manufacturers in North America.

3. The music video for her song "Wait and See" was shot on the former set of TV's *Hannah Montana*. The video featured *Family Matters* star Jaleel White.

4. Camryn had a bit part as a zombie cheerleader in the movie *Judy Moody and the Not Bummer Summer*.

5. In 2012, Billboard featured Camryn as one of its "Bubbling Under" artists, "new and noteworthy acts making their way toward Billboard chart success."

among the largest *Today* has ever seen for its free concert series.

The enormous crowd required additional security and the ensuing pandemonium made folks sit up and take notice. U.S. radio stations began playing 1D's songs with more frequency. They were written about in U.S. magazines and newspapers. Their legion of followers on social network platforms was growing daily. Their debut single, "What Makes You Beautiful," sold more than 100,000 copies in its first weekend and topped the iTunes chart within 13 minutes of being released.

Just 10 days after the band appeared on *Today*, One Direction became the first U.K. group ever to debut at No. 1 on the U.S. Billboard 200 album chart. The band sold 176,000 copies of its debut album, Up All Night, within the first week of its release.

In early 2012, the band announced Australian and North American legs of a 62-date tour. TicketNews reported that tickets to all of 1D's 2012 dates sold out within hours of going on sale. Almost immediately, the price of tickets to these shows doubled and tripled on the secondary market. A front row ticket to the group's June 23, 2012, show in Dallas, for example, was going for more than $1,600.

PERFORMING AT THE O2

Since its opening in 2007, London's O2 Arena has been host to many concerts. It's also where One Direction opened its 2013 Take Me Home Tour on Feb. 23.

Named after its main sponsor, the telecommunications company O2, the arena is located in the middle of The O2 Entertainment Complex on the Greenwich Peninsula. The arena has a capacity of up to 20,000 – depending upon a show's specific stage arrangement. The O2 is the second-largest arena in the United Kingdom (Manchester Arena is bigger) and one of the largest venues in all of Europe.

Sporting events ranging from ice hockey and basketball to gymnastics and mixed martial arts are held at the O2. The multi-purpose arena hosted several events during the 2012 Summer Olympics and 2012 Summer Paralympics; in the context of those events it was referred to as North Greenwich Arena.

The O2 is considered one of the world's premier music venues. Artists including the Rolling Stones, Celine Dion, Beyoncé, Bon Jovi, Katy Perry, Rihanna, Coldplay, Elton John, Lady Gaga, Placido Domingo, Muse, Radiohead and Nicki Minaj have all played the O2 and the Brit Awards have taken place there since 2011.

It's certain that the One Direction guys enjoyed the O2's luxurious backstage hang-out area, complete with a private nightclub-like space, candy dispensers, video games, library, music system and more. Stars can have any kind of food they desire delivered to their private rooms and there's a personal butler available to take on tasks from running errands to booking hotels and restaurants.

Spa-like rooms and on-staff massage therapists are available to help relax stars. There's also a party room where celebs can entertain their guests with luxury furnishings, computer game consoles and private catering.

"When a celebrity arrives for a gig, it will be like checking into the penthouse suite of the Four Seasons," a source told *The (London) Mirror*, shortly after the arena opened. "It's ... like Disneyland for celebrities. They won't want to leave once they get here."

Even before they'd finished their 2012 tour, One Direction announced the band would be headlining a 2013 World Tour, which kicked off February 22 with four shows at London's O2 Arena. Those shows also sold out almost as quickly as tickets became available, oftentimes 12 to 16 months ahead of the actual show.

Noting that 1D will have performed at least 171 live shows by the time they end their tour in New Zealand in October 2013, Andy Greene, associate editor of *Rolling Stone*, said: "I've never known a band to announce a second summer tour before a first summer tour is over. It's insane – they're working them like dogs and printing money right now."

For their part, the guys say they're prepared for the hard work required by non-stop touring. They say they've learned to pace themselves following their 2012 tour, when they all got run down and needed vitamin shots and medical attention. The guys know fans can be fickle and fame can be fleeting; they want to make the very most of this world tour.

UP ALL NIGHT

The full track list for One Direction's debut album:

"What Makes You Beautiful"
"Gotta Be You"
"One Thing"
"More than This"
"Up All Night"
"I Wish"
"Tell Me a Lie"
"Taken"

"I Want"
"Everything About You"
"Same Mistakes"
"Save You Tonight"
"Stole My Heart"
Limited edition yearbook tracks:
"Stand Up"
"Moments"

"The music industry moves so fast, you have to be on your toes," Niall told *We Love Pop* magazine. "Lady Gaga is at the peak of her career, but it could all go from under her. She's stopping that by bringing out song after song and keeping people interested. We're lucky because we've got a good fan base, but if they don't like our music, how long is that going to last?"

To go from being five solo artists competing on a reality show a couple years ago to becoming one of the hottest touring acts around, is both impressive and a little overwhelming. Some highlights, to date, include:

▸ Performing during the closing ceremonies of the 2012 London Olympics.
▸ Meeting Queen Elizabeth II and performing for her at London's Royal Albert Hall.
▸ Convincing British Prime Minister David Cameron to make a cameo appearance in their "One Way or Another (Teenage Kicks)" music video.

▶ Meeting First Lady Michelle Obama and having first daughters, Sasha and Malia, in the audience when they performed in Virginia as part of their first U.S. headline tour.

The 1D guys insist their palms still get sweaty when they meet famous folks and they occasionally can't believe their good fortune.

"We never expected any of this at all," Liam told Sweden TV in July 2012. "We thought that we would do a little bit in the U.S. after the end of the show. Now, it has gone all over the world and more things have happened to us than we would ever have imagined. We owe it all to our fans ... they are incredible and they have got us this far."

Powered by fans, it seems likely that One Direction will continue to soar into the future.

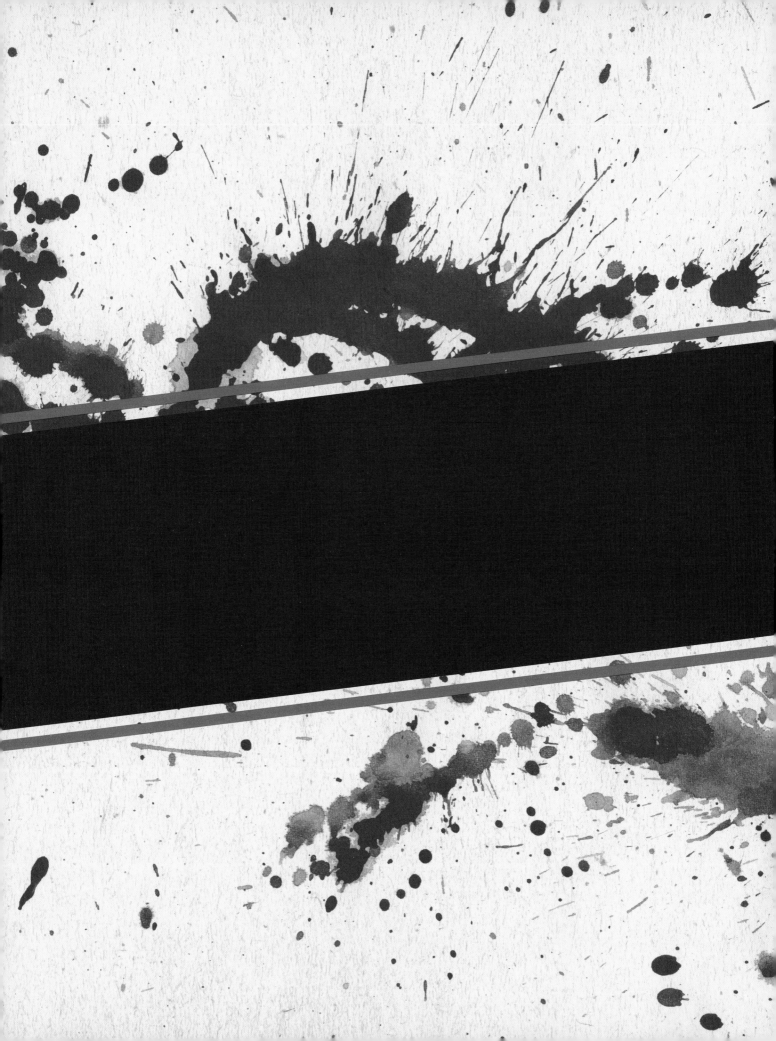

CHAPTER THREE
TAKE ME HOME

One Direction's sophomore album, *Take Me Home*, is not a huge departure from their first – and that's by design. Why, after all, would you mess with success?

"I think it's a bit more mature, for sure," Louis Tomlinson told CBS' *Celebuzz* in October 2012. "Obviously, there aren't that many big changes, but I do think it's just a better album. It does sound a bit more mature. We want the album to grow with us. We're a year older, so our music sounds a bit older, I suppose."

Sure, the drums are a bit heavier, there's a little more guitar and the guys' voices have become stronger, but songwise? Most of the cuts on *Take Me Home* could have fit in on 1D's wildly popular debut CD. As *Billboard* magazine succinctly pointed out in a November 2012 article about One Direction's second album: "They're not out to reinvent the boy band model, but rather

TAKE ME HOME: THE CRITICS REACT

Critics love to criticize. Music critics listen to new albums over and over, often finding fault with the very things fans adore. A beat that seems "redundant" to one listener, for example, will come across as "danceable" to another.

Critics' opinions matter because they generally broadcast their thoughts to a broad audience via newspaper, magazine, radio or Internet.

Here's a sampling of what critics had to say about One Direction's sophomore album, *Take Me Home*:

"The album feels relentless in rhythm, sometimes even during the ballads, with a homogenous sound and message – like a teenage boy who says all the right words in a rush to get what he wants. But this time they're only singing the right words to get to your wallets and adoration. And they're most likely going to get it."

- Cristina Jaleru for Huffingtonpost.com

* * *

"The boy band's sophomore album is pop candy in the purest sense — sweet, colorful, and unlike so many releases aimed at ticklish tweenage hearts, consistent. There's no filler in a bag of Skittles, right? Just Skittles."

- Chris Richards for the *Washington Post*

* * *

"Cuteness-wise, One Direction makes all the other boy bands look like hunchbacks who should've never been let out of the bell tower. That lets them get over as little more than bland song conduits. Their second album rivals the best of Backstreet and 'N Sync when the material pumps (power-pop sure shots like "Kiss You," "Back for You" and the Clash-biting "Live While We're Young," written by masters like Shellback and Rami Yacoub). But when it doesn't (i.e., most of the ballads), a certain amount of douchiness creeps in: "You still have to squeeze into your jeans, but you're perfect to me," one of them sings on "Little Things." Hey, buddy, you're a millionaire: Buy her some loose jeans."

- Jon Dolan for *Rolling Stone*

* * *

"Rest assured, *Take Me Home* is a record destined for commercial success. Since the release of *Up All Night* last March, One Direction has picked up big-time momentum and shows no signs of slowing down any time soon. Next year's world tour was a quick sellout and new single 'Live While We're Young' has already broken the Hot 100 record for the highest debut of a song by a U.K. group. On their new album, they're not out to reinvent the boy band model, but rather perfect it for a 2012 audience that lapped up their debut."

- *Billboard* magazine

* * *

"These may be the least articulate cads on the pop charts, but their beats speak volumes."
- Josh Langhoff for PopMatters.com

* * *

"After leaving U.S. fans without a new album for all of eight months (tween time conversion: 4EVA!!!), the U.K.'s favorite multiplatinum puppy basket are back with even more airtight harmonies and blokes-will-be-blokes cheek. True to their name, 1D haven't veered an inch off course since their debut — catchy new tracks 'Kiss You' and 'Heart Attack' would've fit right in on (March 2012's) *Up All Night*. But the rush shows: most of *Take Me Home* is filler with barely enough zip to keep the kids up past dinner."
- Adam Markovitz for EW.com

BBC RADIO 1'S
TeEN
AWARDS
BBC
RADIO
1
2012
Best British Album
All Night - One Direction

perfect it for a 2012 audience that lapped up their debut."

The group's more-of-same strategy seems to be working.

Take Me Home was released Nov. 9, 2012, by Sony Music Entertainment. According to Nielsen SoundScan, the CD sold 540,000 copies in its first week, giving One Direction its second American No. 1 album of the calendar year.

Only two other 2012 albums sold more copies in their first week of release: Taylor Swift's *Red* with 1.2 million and Mumford & Sons' *Babel* at 600,000. The album topped the charts in more than 35 countries, including the United Kingdom, giving 1D their first No. 1 album in their home country. *Take Me Home* ended 2012 as the fourth best-selling album of the year, selling 4.4 million units.

The first single from the album, "Live While We're Young," also made Billboard chart history. Its 341,000 first-week sales marked the biggest opening week single sales for a non-U.S. artist.

Even as they sit on top of the world, the guys admit they were anxious about how the new album would be received.

"Everyone's said that second albums are the hardest, so before we started recording we were a bit nervous," Harry Styles told media gathered at the 2012 iTunes Festival in London.

Relieved by the project's immediate – and ongoing – success, Harry took to Twitter to express his gratitude: *Hello ...Thank you so*

MEET SAVAN KOTECHA

Savan Kotecha. It's a name One Direction fans should learn and remember.

This American songwriter, producer and talent coach has penned hits including Britney Spears' "If U Seek Amy" and "I Wanna Go," Justin Bieber's "Beauty and a Beat," Usher's "DJ Got Us Fallin' in Love," Carrie Underwoods' "Inside Your Heaven" and Maroon 5's "One More Night."

Kotecha, whose parents worked for IBM, was raised in Austin, Texas. He says he knew from his early teen years that he wanted to be a musician and started writing songs by the time he was 16.

Savan says his parents initially weren't very happy about his career choice.

"We come from a culture where we believe the more education the better it is," Harish Kotecha told India Abroad Publications in 2005. "But when we realized how Savan was serious about his music, we helped to set up a studio at home, and helped him travel and meet musicians and producers."

That support enabled him to ink a deal with BMG Music when he was just 21 years old. Thanks to BMG, Kotecha traveled to Sweden to work with veteran songwriters RedOne, Kristian Lundin and Max Martin. At the same time, he began to build a working relationship with Simon Cowell, who brought on Kotecha as a consultant for his label, Syco Records.

Kotecha began working with One Direction when they were contestants on *The X Factor*. He was a vocal coach, mentoring them throughout the competition's live shows. He also wrote their hit single "What Makes You Beautiful."

Kotecha says he'd messed around with the melody of the chorus for that song for about a year until he was in a hotel room in London with his wife and she was having a bad morning.

"She was like, 'Oh, I feel so ugly' and I was like, 'No, you look beautiful. You don't know how beautiful you look.' And I was like, 'Oh, crap! That's a good song! Hold on!'" he told *The Hollywood Reporter* in early 2013.

Kotecha had helped develop 1D's sound on *The X Factor* and thought the song might be a good fit for them.

"I knew what they were capable of and what they could do," he said. "And 'What Makes You Beautiful' is just one of those, you know, lightning strikes."

Lightning has continued to strike for the 34-year-old super songwriter. He's since written or co-written a handful of other songs for the 1D team, including "Live While We're Young," "Na Na Na," "I Wish," "Up All Night," "Save You Tonight," "Kiss You," "One Thing," "I Want," "Heart Attack," "Last First Kiss," "Back for You," "Nobody Compares," "Still the One," "Change My Mind" and "Magic."

much for all your support with this album. We can't believe the number ones today! Thank you thank you. Huge Love. xx

Rock-infused pop, vocal harmonies, hand claps and electric guitar riffs are commonalities found throughout the album's 13 tracks. Lyrics touch on many love-related themes: falling in love, unrequited love, jealousy, loyalty and lost love.

Songwriter/producer Carl Falk and his songwriting/producing partner, Rami Yacoub, produced three songs ("What Makes You Beautiful," "One Thing" and "I Wish") for One Direction's debut album.

The 1D guys traveled to Falk's hometown of Stockholm, Sweden, where they did much of the composing and recording for *Take Me Home.*

Falk told *The (London) Examiner* in May 2012 that 1D's album is an update rather than a reinvention.

"It would be stupid of us to go completely different with the new songs when you have a successful band," he said, noting that the guys' singing voices have gotten both deeper and stronger since recording their first album.

"Groups like One Direction need to have identity in their voices. If they all sounded

TAKE ME HOME

The full track list for One Direction's sophomore album:

"Live While We're Young"
"Kiss You"
"Little Things"
"C'mon, C'mon"
"Last First Kiss"
"Heart Attack"
"Rock Me"

"Change My Mind"
"I Would"
"Over Again"
"Back for You"
"They Don't Know About Us"
"Summer Love"

the same, it wouldn't be interesting," he said. "They have really, really different character in their voices. We were really impressed with how they delivered on the second album, compared to the first album.

"On the first album they were a little more insecure and they didn't really know their voices that well. But, at this point, they have better character in their voices. They knew what they were good at, and they knew what other members of the group could do better. It was a smooth and really easy process for us to record this time."

Falk identified the specific musical strength that each of the guys brings to One Direction:

▶ **Niall Horan.** Need to hit a high note? He's your man. Niall's range has improved over time and the group's record producers say his deep voice sounds better than ever.

▶ **Zayn Malik.** His clean, tenor voice is well suited for pop or rhythm and blues. Zayn handles many of the group's

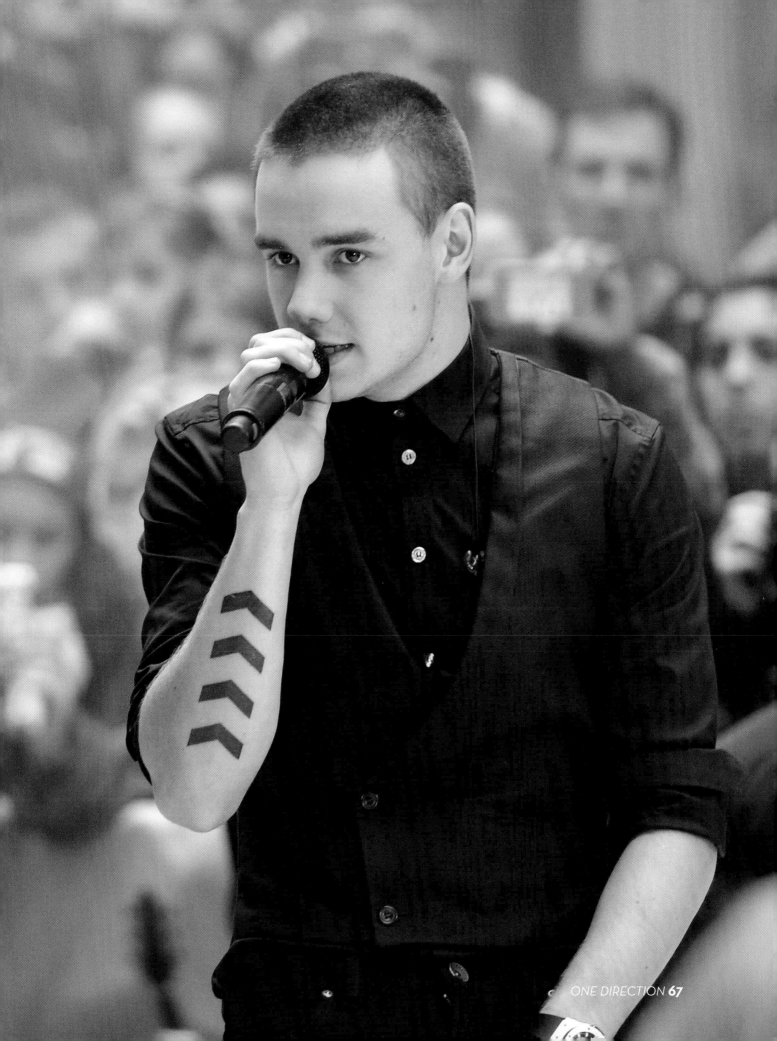

runs and more soulful ad libs.

▶ **Liam Payne.** He sings many of the group's lower solo parts (check out the beginning of "Live While We're Young.") You will also hear Liam singing some falsetto along the way.

▶ **Harry Styles.** His voice is raw and raspy – a good contrast to the other guys, whose sounds are crisper and cleaner.

▶ **Louis Tomlinson.** The highest tenor of the group, Louis provides a great complement to Harry's huskier voice. Louis' voice is pure and sounds terrific when belting out sorrowful lyrics (think heartbreak).

With each group member becoming more aware of his strengths – and weaknesses – the guys are now better able to work together. They've all become more confident about offering ideas and feedback.

Still, when it comes time to decide who will be featured and who will sing solos on various songs, Falk says it's very much a matter of experimentation.

"We record the parts that we think could

TAKE ME TO WHICH HOME?

One Direction's second album shares its name with some other fairly popular recordings. This is your warning: If you don't tell grandma exactly which *Take Me Home* you want, she may buy you one of these:

▶ Jack Savoretti's 2012 "Take Me Home" is a single from his CD *Before the Storm*. This Italian-English acoustic artist's songwriting skills have been compared to those of Simon and Garfunkel and industry insiders have called him the "new Bob Dylan."

▶ Celtic Thunder's 2009 *Take Me Home* is a 16-song CD. The Irish vocal quintet performs a blend of traditional and contemporary tunes including "Green Fields of France," "Midnight Well" and "You Raise Me Up."

▶ Zox's 2003 *Take Me Home* album was released in 2003. Zox is based in Providence, R.I., and is self-described as "violin-laced reggae rock."

▶ Ale'a's 2000 *Take Me Home* was released by Poki Records. The four Hawaiian musicians who form this group combined forces while playing for island tourists in 1997. As winners of a Battle for the Bash competition, Ale'a won a recording contract; their resulting debut album was honored as Best Island Contemporary Album of the Year.

▶ The Bellamy Brothers 1995 *Take Me Home* was released by Intersound Records. The Bellamy Brothers are a

pop/country music duo from Darby, Fla. The real-life brothers had considerable musical success in the 1970s and 1980s.

▸ Cher's 1979 *Take Me Home* was the 15th studio album recorded by the American singer-actress. The record was produced by Bob Esty and Ron Dante and marked the beginning of Cher's brief venture into disco music.

be good for any of the guys," he says. "We let them try solos on each song, for the most part. And we end up recording it, so we end up having different options. And then, when we edit the vocals, we compare them and ask: 'Who sings this best?' So we make sure we have options. No one gets left out. Everyone gets a chance to sing a solo."

As agreeable as the guys typically are, Niall says there's no clear-cut favorite when it comes to *Take Me Home* tracks.

"We all have our individual favorites, we're never going to have the same," he told interviewer Ryan Seacrest in November 2012. "A song called 'Little Things,' it's like an acoustic ballad. That seems to be one that everyone likes."

"Little Things" joins "I Would," "Over Again" and "Kiss You" as critics' favorites.

The fans? They love it all. And why wouldn't they? *Take Me Home* stays true to One Direction's rollicking pop sounds and, best of all, the guys are still completely swoon-worthy.

CHAPTER FOUR
ON THE BIG SCREEN

Hearing the One Direction guys sing is great. Reading about them is informative. Dancing to their melodic tunes is just plain fun.

Watching them on the big screen? Now, that's going to be phenomenal.

This Is Us, a fun, behind-the-scenes movie about One Direction, is set for release on August 30, 2013.

The theatrical release will be part concert, part documentary. The film follows Harry Styles, Zayn Malik, Niall Horan, Liam Payne and Louis Tomlinson as they launch their world tour. "You think you know their story, but this is just the beginning," reads the film's title card.

The movie, which previously had the working title *1D3D* comes from TriStar Pictures (Sony). It promises to include interview snippets with the guys and their families. You'll also see the lads partying with supermodels, hanging out

IT ALL ADDS UP FOR ONE DIRECTION

1	Number of Guinness World Records the band holds. The honor celebrates the fact that 1D became the first British group in U.S. chart history to score a No. 1 hit with its debut release.
2	Number of One Direction albums among 2012's five best sellers.
3	The place in which One Direction finished during the seventh season of *The X Factor.*
40	Number of countries in which "Live While We're Young" went to the top of the pre-order charts.
49	Number of tattoos the guys have – for now.
53	Number of awards the band had racked up through March 2013. (The band had 19 pending award nominations at the time this book went to press, so expect that number to grow.)
77	Number of times One Direction sings the word "Na" in their song "Na Na Na."
117	Number of shows on 1D's 2013 *Take Me Home* World Tour.
176,000	Number of copies *Up All Night* sold in the United States during its first week of release.
540,000	Number of copies of the band's sophomore effort, *Take Me Home*, sold in the U.S. during its first week of release.
49,048,544	Number of Twitter followers on the five guys' individual accounts combined. One Direction's official group account has an additional 10.5 million followers.
347,666,429	Number of YouTube views of the group's August 2011 video "What Makes You Beautiful."

with A-listers, signing autographs, joking and playing, and there will be lots and lots of screaming fans. The movie goes everywhere the guys go – even to the bathroom.

"The fans know us," Niall told *The (London) Sun.* "But we want them to know us deeper."

The guys don't seem to be too worried about giving cameras unlimited access, perhaps because they are in the very capable hands of director Morgan Spurlock.

Spurlock is one of the most well-known documentary filmmakers working in Hollywood. He was nominated for an Academy Award for 2004's *Super Size Me.* Spurlock's second feature documentary,

Where in the World Is Osama Bin Laden? premiered at the Sundance Film Festival in 2008. *Freakonomics* and *The Greatest Movie Ever Sold* also are among his more well-known films.

"This is an incredible opportunity and an amazing moment in time for the band," Spurlock told *The (London) Guardian.* "To capture this journey and share it with audiences around the world will be an epic undertaking that I am proud to be a part of."

Given Spurlock's background, it is likely a good portion of the movie will focus on One Direction fans and their obsession with the handsome lads.

Harry says shooting the movie in 3D provides a chance for fans to feel like

they're getting closer to the band. "My hair (will) be poking in your eye," he joked to *The Sun*.

In addition to Spurlock's professional crew, Niall has revealed that he's also been entrusted with a camera to shoot some of the movie while 1D is on its *Take Me Home Tour*.

Between all the jokes and pranks, there are parts of the movie where the guys get serious about the close bonds they've built with each other. "I always wanted a little brother and now I've got four of them," says Liam.

One person you won't see in *This is Us*

is singer Taylor Swift. According to *Life & Style*, the film crew shot footage of Taylor and Harry during their brief romance. Now that the two are no longer a couple, sources claim Harry has asked that those scenes be deleted from the movie.

The insider explained: "During their two-month relationship, producers shot Taylor and Harry in LA and NYC last year, but Harry has ordered that none of it make the final cut. (Harry) wants nothing more to do with Taylor. It was a fling and it's done."

Upon seeing a sneak peak of the Taylor-less flick, *The X Factor* executive producer Simon Cowell tweeted: "One Direction

TWITTER ME THIS

Y ou follow them all, but do you pay close enough attention to tell Harry's tweets from Niall's and Zayn's? Liam's from Louis'? Here's a chance to put your 1D Twitter knowledge to the test. Which group member sent out which tweets? Here's a hint, we've included three tweets from each of the guys:

1.   "Since using Twitter I find I try to use the shortest sentences possible. All the time. Sometimes you need 141 characters." Tweeted by _____

2.   "Okay bored of constant news articles ... I'm not dating Leona... My YouTube channel isn't for a solo career and I didn't insult Kim K... Pow!" Tweeted by _____

3.   "I actually can't believe people actually believe that our security carry guns? Biggest load of sh*& I've ever heard. Ha. :)" Tweeted by _____

4.   "Yawn!" Tweeted by _____

5.   "Clearly some people are not very familiar with flirting." Tweeted by _____

6.   "Thank you so much Manchester ... Amazing crowd tonight. And to the person eat-

ing a kabob during the show, you're my hero." Tweeted by _____

7.   "Just imagine if KFC was healthy and you could eat as much as you want!!" Tweeted by _____

8.   "I was not in a crash and that is not my car." Tweeted by _____

9.   "I love the 'Cash Cab' TV show!! Ha, it's sick!!" Tweeted by _____

10.   "First rule of One Direction rehearsals, if in doubt ... Spread out." Tweeted by _____

11.   "Watchin' 'Skyfall!' I reckon I'm the next Bond! Don't mess with me, I just started growin' a little chin hair!" Tweeted by _____

12.   "I am the slowest YouTuber ever ... If I don't sort it out soon, I'm gonna get a slap on the beeeeehind. Ahh." Tweeted by _____

13.   "In life we always fall for the person that will never fall for us, always want something that we can't (have) and always say things we shouldn't. :s" Tweeted by _____

14.   "Got in yesterday, spilled a full tub of pasta on the floor. Stupid, stupid, stupid-dddddd boy. Smelly pasta house." Tweeted by _____

15.   "Just goin' for a quick power nap! I'm knackered." Tweeted by _____

continue to amaze me. Hard workers but still the nicest guys you could hope to work with." It should be noted that Cowell is one of the movie's producers.

Industry insiders speculate the members of One Direction stand to make millions from the movie, though exactly how much is unclear; the *Sun* even published two separate articles about the movie on the same day and listed different dollar figures in each. In one article, the newspaper reported that each of the five band members would make $10.4 million from the movie; the other article reported each musician would pocket a cool $16 million for the film.

This is Us is hardly the first music-centric documentary. In fact, here are a few others you may want to check out:

Woodstock. This 1970 film documents the 1969 Woodstock music festival. More than 120 miles of raw footage gave editors a chance to choose the very best scenes. Oh, and the editing team was headed up by someone you've probably heard of — Martin Scorsese.

Truth or Dare. This 1991 film chronicles the life of Madonna during her Blond Ambition World Tour; it is the eighth-highest grossing documentary of all time. Onstage concert footage is shown in color but the rest of the documentary was done in black and white. Along the way, moviegoers see Madonna try to come to grips with technical difficulties, disagreements with her crew, throat problems and a heart-wrenching trip to her hometown of Detroit.

Bad25. This TV documentary, produced by Spike Lee, celebrates the 25th anniversary of Michael Jackson's *Bad* album release and tour. The film includes interviews with folks including Quincy Jones, Martin Scorsese and even Jackson himself. A longer version of the documentary was released on DVD in early 2013.

Searching for Sugar Man. This movie, by Swedish filmmaker Malik Bendjelloul, tells the story of Sixto Rodriguez, an American singer/songwriter whose music never became popular in the States but

who was a huge star in South Africa. The documentary details the efforts of two Cape Town fans who wanted to learn what had happened to their idol. The film was named 2013 Best Documentary at the British Academy Awards and Best Documentary Feature at the 85th Academy Awards in Hollywood.

Katy Perry: Part of Me. This music documentary chronicles Katy Perry's year-long California Dreams World Tour in 2011. The movie contains personal interviews, film of the very energetic Perry interacting with her fans, and lots of concert footage. There's talk about the singer's religious upbringing, her unusual costume choices and her relationship with actor Russell Brand.

Justin Bieber: Never Say Never. This documentary follows Justin Bieber during the days leading up to his sold-out show at Madison Square Garden in August 2010. The film includes footage of concerts and rehearsals, interspersed with home movies, interviews and old photos.

CHAPTER FIVE

ONE DIRECTION FANS ROCK

There are many nights when One Direction's overzealous fans get so carried away that dozens of pairs of panties end up onstage. The lobbing of lingerie actually amuses the guys.

"We've nearly fallen over knickers on stage," joked Liam Payne.

"I like knickers," added Harry Styles.

Underwear is one thing, but when fans get so wound up they start tossing bigger, heavier, harder objects – well, that can pose a problem.

Such was the case at One Direction's February 26, 2013, concert in Glasgow, Scotland. The pop stars were chatting up the crowd when – BAM – out of nowhere, a shoe came flying onto the stage. Harry picked it up and announced to the audience, "It's a shoe."

Just then, the other shoe dropped ... or rather dropped Harry – hitting him squarely in the crotch. The floppy-haired

singer doubled-over and fell to the floor. Fortunately, no real damage was done and Harry was back on his feet in no time.

A day later, the shoe-thrower took to Twitter to apologize: "tonight i threw my shoe and it hit harry in the (groin) then security came and took me out (of) the concert then i got my shoe back hahahaha." She indicated that after security escorted her from the concert hall, Harry sent word to have them let her back in. To Styles, she tweeted, "i never meant to hurt you."

The One Direction guys say the tossing of undies and footwear is just a sampling of the sometimes crazed behavior they see from their fans.

Louis Tomlinson recounted for *OK!*

magazine a time when a young Italian fan recognized the guys, so they stopped to have their photo taken with her.

"Then out of pure randomness I decided to splat my ice-cream on her face – and she kept it there," he said. "I saw her two hours later at our signing and she still hadn't wiped it off!"

Ireland, England, Scotland, Australia, Japan – One Direction has fans all over the globe. But when it comes to volume, the pop stars say their U.S. fans are among the loudest.

More than 10,000 screaming fans showed up for 1D's first American television concert in March 2012. In Nashville, dozens of girls chased the band's car down Music Row. In Natick, Mass., fans swarmed to

SMILE! ONE DIRECTION MERCHANDISE IS PLENTIFUL

Fans eager to grab hold of One Direction and squ-ee-zz-ee can actually do that now. No, don't grab the actual guys! But you can buy a tube of One Direction toothpaste and squeeze it all you want – preferably from the end, but that's up to you.

One Direction teamed up with Colgate to put their faces on a line of Colgate MaxFresh products. The One Direction Colgate MaxFresh Power Toothbrush (with a small oscillating head), One Direction Colgate MaxFresh Manual Toothbrush, and One Direction Colgate MaxFresh Toothpaste hit store shelves in November 2012.

Minty fresh One Direction-inspired breath is just one reason fans have to smile. A wide array of 1D merchandise is now available to fans around the globe.

You can decorate your room with One Direction stickers, posters, door hangers, clocks, sheets, comforters and pillows. The guys can go to school with you if you invest in a 1D lunch box, pencil case or backpack. Prefer to take them to the beach? Just get yourself a One Direction swim cover-up or towel.

The boys' handsome mugs are also on everything from T-shirts and hoodies to key rings and phone cases.

Toymaker Vivid Imaginations even put out a line of One Direction dolls for Christmas 2011 in the United Kingdom; by spring 2012, Hasbro had released the collection in the United States.

The dolls, which measure 12 to 13 inches tall, cost $27 to $43 each and are outfitted to look just like the real thing. The Louis doll, for instance, is dressed in his trademark striped shirt and the Zayn doll is wearing a red letterman-style jacket.

Can't decide between Harry and Niall? Buy them all and stage a doll-sized concert in your bedroom.

If dolls aren't your thing, perhaps you'll instead be drawn to one of these impressively unusual 1D gems:

▶ One Direction Ice Pops. These frozen, fruit-flavored gems come wrapped in packaging emblazoned with cartoonish images of Niall, Zayn, Liam, Harry and Louis. Finding this tasty summer treat may be a trick in the United States, but they're widely available in the United Kingdom.

▶ Smells like One Direction. In a partnership with Olivann Beauty, One Direction announced it will be releasing its first fragrance in fall 2013.

▶ 1D UGGs. These colorful UGG boots come in a variety of pastel shades and contain a large "1D" logo on the calf. Not into twin-face sheepskin boots? The UGG company has announced that it's also releasing a line of One Direction flip flops, shorts, shirts and more.

▶ 1D Floor Mat. This 100 percent cotton 3-by-5-foot rug proclaims "I (Heart) One

Direction". Decorated in strips of purple, pink, blue and green, this sign of your fandom would look great in any bedroom or bathroom.

▶ One Direction Hot Water Bottle Cover. Feeling sick and achy? Cuddle up with this snazzy red hot water bottle cover and you'll be feeling better in no time. This item, sold directly by OneDirectionStore.com, does not include the water bottle.

a shopping mall when the guys held an autograph session there. And more than 100 security guards had to be hired to protect the guys when they performed a show at Dallas' Dr. Pepper Park.

"The fans (in the United States) are really loud and crazy," Niall Horan told *The (London) Mirror*. "When we're in the tour bus, they start climbing all over it and smacking on the windows, trying to get in. They start chasing after us, screaming... One girl was like an Olympic sprinter. She followed us for about five blocks to our hotel. She was unbelievably fit."

Musician Olly Murs, who spent six weeks opening shows for 1D, has his own loyal fans but that didn't keep him from being surprised by the crowds that greeted them throughout their U.S. tour.

"It was the first time I have ever been in front of One Direction's fan base and I have never seen anything like it," Murs told Kent (England) Online. "Girls were running after the buses. It was quite dangerous at times, they are insane but their response was amazing ... It was very loud."

One Direction is always quick to express their love and gratitude to fans. If it weren't for fans, after all, they wouldn't be where they are. But there are certainly times

THE WANTED VS. 1D

One Direction fans love their British boy band. The Wanted fans love their British boy band. But fans rarely love both bands – perhaps because there's no love lost between the two groups.

Back in March 2012, members of the two musical acts seemed to be getting along swimmingly. "We all know each other. It's the same in the U.K. as it is here. Everyone knows each other," Niall Horan told MTV News. "We haven't seen The Wanted in a while. We just haven't been in the same place at the same time. They're really nice guys. And every time we've met them, we've had a good laugh with them. The more, the merrier! Let's bring the British invasion over here and show them what we got."

In the months since that very public expression of brotherly love, things have gotten, well, downright ugly.

Blame The Wanted, say the 1D guys. They started things by "badmouthing" One Direction in the press.

"We're not bothered about the friction or the rivalry," Louis Tomlinson told *Now* magazine in November 2012. "But I'm not going to shy away from it, because that isn't the person I am. I don't think it's fair to me or any of the lads."

Things really heated up when Zayn Malik and The Wanted's Max George got into it on Twitter:

Max: "Psy and me getting messy #geekandproud"

Zayn: "The first step is totally acceptance. #geekoftheweek. You display just how much of a wannabe you are. :)"

Max: "That's not very nice, @ZaynMalik. I was just starting to like you and your RnB songs, too."

Before you could sing a quick "Na na na," a full-fledged Twitter war had broken out – with additional band members and fans hurling insults at one another.

"Zayn Malik had his '1 Stripes' knickers in a twist, bro" tweeted Tom Parker of The Wanted.

"Pipe down bad boy" tweeted Louis Tomlinson.

"Sorry 'sass master'" responded Parker.

"@TheWantedMusic I don't know why you give One Direction s**t, you can't even sing. Glee did a better version of your song than you #yousuck" tweeted a 1D fan.

The Twitter war raged on for a while; the most inflammatory comments have since been deleted. Max was still outraged enough in December 2012 to tell journalists he'd be happy to fight the One Direction guys – even if it meant getting arrested.

While the two groups continue to hurl insults toward each other, music lovers seem to be the ones benefitting. Author Toba Beta once said: "Competition is a rude, yet effective motivation." In this case, each group is being motivated to outperform the other, resulting in some really, really great music.

when the guys wish their admirers would calm down just a notch.

In March 2012, Niall told a *Digital Spy* reporter: "You can see girls getting too excited and they start crying or worse. In a lot of these countries they don't get a lot of gigs to go to, so when they get to see their favorite artist, they take full advantage of it. Obviously the excitement builds up too much for some on the night and they get a bit ... crazy. Sometimes I've seen some stuff that's a bit too much!"

In a February 2013 interview with *The*

(London) Examiner, Zayn Malik described a situation in which he and Louis were lounging poolside when suddenly girls started coming out of the bushes. "It was like something out of a zombie film," he said. "We were like 'What are we going to do?' We found a door that had an entrance back into the hotel and we legged it, being chased by all these girls."

The guys understand that fans are excited and they recognize that the out-of-control ones are in the minority. Directioners who show their love by

wearing 1D T-shirts, carrying banners or setting up fan sites are much more the norm.

Liam says the guys are especially touched when fans bring gifts or write notes that refer to specific items or moments they've mentioned in interviews.

"(Fans) read what we say then send us things we mention," he told *The (London) Mirror*. "I get sent loads of Toy Story Woodie dolls because I once mentioned I liked him."

In fact, Liam insists that – despite occasional lapses in good judgment – their ultra-dedicated fans are a real blessing.

"It's very flattering, obviously, as we can see how much they care for us. We just hope they're crying tears of joy!" he said of their oftentimes tearful fan encounters. "I don't think there is anything hard about having such a dedicated fan base. It is actually great to know that there are people out there that love what we do since we put so much hard work into it. The pressure to not disappoint them is obviously there!"

Bandmate Harry expressed a similar sentiment in an interview with *The (London) Daily*: "We're five normal lads given this massive opportunity and know that without the fans we'd be nowhere. We feel incredibly grateful."

And so do One Direction fans. Grateful, indeed.

DO YOU KNOW YOUR ONE DIRECTION LYRICS?

You hum along to every One Direction tune, but do you pay attention to the lyrics? Match these lines to their respective songs. Answers are at the bottom.

1. The way that you flip your hair gets me overwhelmed.
2. Let's go crazy, crazy, crazy 'til we see the sun.
3. Katy Perry's on replay, she's on replay.
4. Everytime we touch, you get this kinda rush.
5. That little twinkle in your eye gets me every time.
6. It's like I'm finally awake and you're just a beautiful mistake.
7. Got your voice in my head, sayin' "Let's just be friends."
8. Make the last time just like the first time, push a button and rewind.
9. My judgment's clouded like tonight's night sky.
10. Oh girl, can we try one more, one more time?
11. I would swim all the oceans just to see you smile.
12. He looks at you the way that I would. Does all the things I know that I could.
13. You're so pretty when you cry.
14. I'm just the underdog who finally got the girl.
15. He drives to school every morning, while I walk alone in the rain.

a. "Summer Love"
b. "Gotta Be You"
c. "What Makes You Beautiful"
d. "Kiss You"
e. "I Would"
f. "I Wish"
g. "Nobody Compares"
h. "Taken"
i. "Live While We're Young"
j. "Up All Night"
k. "Moments"
l. "Truly Madly Deeply"
m. "Stand Up"
n. "Tell Me a Lie"
o. "Heart Attack"

Answers: 1-c; 2-i; 3-j; 4-d; 5-n; 6-h; 7-o; 8-a; 9-k; 10-b; 11-m; 12-f; 13-g; 14-l; 15-e

ONE DIRECTION 2013 WORLD TOUR

2/23/13	O2 Arena, London, England
2/24/13	O2 Arena, London, England
2/26/13	Scottish Exhibition and Conference Centre, Glasgow, Scotland
2/27/13	Scottish Exhibition and Conference Centre, Glasgow, Scotland
3/1/13	Motorpoint Arena, Cardiff, Wales
3/2/13	Motorpoint Arena, Cardiff, Wales
3/5/13	The O2, Dublin, Ireland
3/6/13	The O2, Dublin, Ireland
3/7/13	Odyssey Arena, Belfast, Northern Ireland
3/8/13	Odyssey Arena, Belfast, Northern Ireland
3/10/13	Odyssey Arena, Belfast, Northern Ireland
3/11/13	Odyssey Arena, Belfast, Northern Ireland
3/12/13	The O2, Dublin, Ireland
3/13/13	The O2, Dublin, Ireland
3/16/13	Manchester Arena, Manchester, England
3/17/13	Echo Arena, Liverpool, England
3/19/13	Motorpoint Arena, Sheffield, England
3/20/13	Capital FM Arena, Nottingham, England
3/22/13	LG Arena, Birmingham, England
3/23/13	LG Arena, Birmingham, England
3/31/13	Echo Arena, Liverpool, England
4/1/13	O2 Arena, London, England
4/2/13	O2 Arena, London, England
4/6/13	O2 Arena, London, England
4/8/13	Metro Radio Arena, Newcastle, England
4/9/13	Metro Radio Arena, Newcastle, England
4/10/13	Metro Radio Arena, Newcastle, England
4/12/13	Scottish Exhibition and Conference Centre, Glasgow, Scotland
4/13/13	Motorpoint Arena, Sheffield, England
4/14/13	Motorpoint Arena, Sheffield, England
4/16/13	Capital FM Arena, Nottingham, England
4/17/13	LG Arena, Birmingham, England
4/19/13	Manchester Arena, Manchester, England
4/29/13	Palais Omnisports, Paris, France

4/30/13	Galaxie Amneville, Amneville, France
5/1/13	Sportpaleis, Antwerp, Belgium
5/3/13	Ziggo Dome, Amsterdam, The Netherlands
5/4/13	Konig Pilsener Arena, Oberhausen, Germany
5/5/13	Jyske Bank Boxen, Herning, Denmark
5/7/13	Telenor Arena, Baerum, Norway
5/8/13	Friends Arena, Stockholm, Sweden
5/10/13	Parken Stadium, Copenhagen, Denmark
5/11/13	O2 World, Berlin, Germany
5/12/13	O2 World Hamburg, Hamburg, Germany
5/16/13	Hallenstadion, Zurich, Switzerland
5/17/13	Olympiahalle, Munich, Germany
5/19/13	Verona Arena, Verona, Italy
5/20/13	Mediolanum Forum, Milan, Italy
5/22/13	Pavello Olumpic de Badalona, Barcelona, Spain
5/25/13	Palacio Vistalegre, Madrid, Spain
5/26/13	Pavilhao Atlantico, Lisbon, Portugal
6/8/13	Foro Sol, Mexico City, Mexico
6/9/13	Foro Sol, Mexico City, Mexico
6/13/13	BB&T Center, Sunrise, Fla.
6/14/13	American Airlines Arena, Miami, Fla.
6/16/13	KFC Yum! Center, Louisville, Ky.
6/18/13	Nationwide Arena, Columbus, Ohio
6/19/13	Bridgestone Arena, Nashville, Tenn.
6/21/13	Philips Arena, Atlanta, Ga.
6/22/13	PNC Arena, Raleigh, N.C.
6/23/13	Verizon Center, Washington, D.C.
6/25/13	Wells Fargo Center, Philadelphia, Penn.
6/26/13	Comcast Center, Mansfield, Mass.
6/28/13	Nikon at Jones Beach Theater, Wantagh, N.Y.
6/29/13	Nikon at Jones Beach Theater, Wantagh, N.Y.
7/2/13	Izod Center, East Rutherford, N.J.
7/4/13	Bell Centre, Montreal, Canada
7/5/13	Hersheypark Stadium, Hershey, Penn.
7/6/13	Hersheypark Stadium, Hershey, Penn.
7/8/13	Consol Energy Center, Pittsburgh, Penn.
7/9/13	Air Canada Centre, Toronto, Canada
7/10/13	Air Canada Centre, Toronto, Canada

7/12/13	Palace Of Auburn Hills, Auburn Hills, Mich.
7/13/13	First Midwest Bank Amphitheatre, Tinley Park, Ill.
7/14/13	First Midwest Bank Amphitheatre, Tinley Park, Ill.
7/18/13	Target Center, Minneapolis, Minn.
7/19/13	Sprint Center, Kansas City, Mo.
7/21/13	Toyota Center, Houston, Texas
7/22/13	American Airlines Center, Dallas, Texas
7/24/13	Pepsi Center, Denver, Colo.
7/25/13	Maverik Center, Salt Lake City, Utah
7/27/13	Rogers Arena, Vancouver, Canada
7/28/13	Key Arena, Seattle, Wash.
7/30/13	HP Pavilion, San Jose, Calif.
7/31/13	Oracle Arena, Oakland, Calif.
8/2/13	Mandalay Bay Events Center, Las Vegas, Nev.
8/3/13	Mandalay Bay Events Center, Las Vegas, Nev.
8/4/13	Cricket Wireless Amphitheatre, Chula Vista, Calif.
8/6/13	Cricket Wireless Amphitheatre, Chula Vista, Calif.
8/7/13	Staples Center, Los Angeles, Calif.
8/8/13	Staples Center, Los Angeles, Calif.
8/9/13	Staples Center, Los Angeles, Calif.
8/10/13	Staples Center, Los Angeles, Calif.
9/23/13	Adelaide Entertainment Centre, Adelaide, Australia
9/24/13	Adelaide Entertainment Centre, Adelaide, Australia
9/25/13	Adelaide Entertainment Centre, Adelaide, Australia
9/28/13	Perth Arena, Perth, Australia
9/29/13	Perth Arena, Perth, Australia
10/2/13	Rod Laver Arena, Melbourne, Australia
10/3/13	Rod Laver Arena, Melbourne, Australia
10/5/13	Allphones Arena, Sydney, Australia
10/6/13	Allphones Arena, Sydney, Australia
10/10/13	CBS Canterbury Arena, Christchurch, New Zealand
10/12/13	Vector Arena, Auckland, New Zealand
10/13/13	Vector Arena, Auckland, New Zealand
10/16/13	Rod Laver Arena, Melbourne, Australia
10/17/13	Rod Laver Arena, Melbourne, Australia
10/19/13	Brisbane Entertainment Centre, Brisbane, Australia
10/20/13	Brisbane Entertainment Centre, Brisbane, Australia
10/21/13	Brisbane Entertainment Centre, Brisbane, Australia

10/23/13	Allphones Arena, Sydney, Australia
10/24/13	Allphones Arena, Sydney, Australia
10/25/13	Allphones Arena, Sydney, Australia
10/26/13	Allphones Arena, Sydney, Australia
10/28/13	Rod Laver Arena, Melbourne, Australia
10/29/13	Rod Laver Arena, Melbourne, Australia
10/30/13	Rod Laver Arena, Melbourne, Australia
11/2/13	Makuhari Messe, Tokyo, Japan
11/3/13	Makuhari Messe, Tokyo, Japan